To the reader:

Welcome to the DK ELT Graded Readers! These readers are different. They explore aspects of the world around us: its history, geography, science ... and a lot of other things. And they show the different ways in which people live now, and lived in the past.

These DK ELT Graded Readers give you material for reading for information, and reading for pleasure. You are using your English to do something real. The illustrations will help you understand the text, and also help bring the Reader to life. There is a glossary to help you understand the special words for this topic. Listen to the cassette or CD as well, and you can really enter the world of the Olympic Games, the *Titanic*, or the Trojan War ... and a lot more. Choose the topics that interest you, improve your English, and learn something ... all at the same time.
Enjoy the series!

To the teacher:

This series provides varied reading practice at five levels of language difficulty, from elementary to FCE level:
BEGINNER
ELEMENTARY A
ELEMENTARY B
INTERMEDIATE
UPPER INTERMEDIATE
The language syllabus has been designed to suit the factual nature of the series, and includes a wider vocabulary range than is usual with ELT readers: language linked with the specific theme of each book is included and glossed. The language scheme, and ideas for exploiting the material (including the recorded material) both in and out of class are contained in the Teacher's Resource Book.
We hope you and your students enjoy using this series.

DK

A DORLING KINDERSLEY BOOK

[DK] www.dk.com

Originally published as Eyewitness Reader
Volcanoes and Other Natural Disasters in 1998
and adapted as an ELT Graded Reader for
Dorling Kindersley by

studio cactus ⊙

13 SOUTHGATE STREET WINCHESTER HAMPSHIRE SO23 9DZ

Published in Great Britain by
Dorling Kindersley Limited
9 Henrietta Street, London WC2E 8PS

2 4 6 8 10 9 7 5 3 1

Copyright © 2000
Dorling Kindersley Limited, London

A CIP catalogue record for this book is
available from the British Library.

ISBN: 0-7513-3173-2

Colour reproduction by Colourscan, Singapore
Printed and bound in China
by L. Rex Printing Co., Ltd
Text film output by Ocean Colour, UK

The publisher would like to thank the following for their kind
permission to reproduce their photographs:
t = top, b = bottom, l = left, r = right, c = centre, m = middle

Andes Press Agency 38tl, 41tr (Caretas); Arquivo Fotografico 15t;
Barnaby's Picture Library/F Newman 45t; The Bridgeman Art Library
14b; Andrew Burgess 7cr; Camera Press 4 tl, 20b; Circus World
Museum 23b; Colorific!/Penny Tweedie 5bl, 43t; Corbis-
Bettman/Reuters 45b; Corbis-Bettmann/UPI 4 bl, 22t, 27t, 28-29,
31t, 34t 35b, 36tl 37tr, 41br; Lin Esposito 3c, 6bl, 7tr, 33br; Mary
Evans Picture Library 4cr, 9t, 15cl 16-17, 22b, 30ml 5rb, 33bl;
Robert Harding Picture Library 4cl, 14t (Guy Motil), Hulton Getty
33b, 26t; Library of Congress 30-1bl; Ingrid Morejohn/Picture Works
18b, 20t; Pictor International, 26b; Planet Earth Pictures 4 br, 23tl,
24cl; Rex Features 19m; Science Photo Library/ NASA 32 cl;
South American Pictures/ Tony Morrison 38cl; Frank Spooner
Pictures 5cr (Brian Morrison), 46tr (Bouvet/Hires/Duclos) 46b
(Fornaciari-Nosca); Tony Stone Images 42bl (Ian Murphy), 42tr
(Margaret Gowan); The Stock Market 4 bm, 40 (Ned Gillette),
5tr, Sygma 9b (De Grucy) 48t, 19t; Telegraph Colour Library 33cr,
47br; Topham Picture Point 13, 23tr; Wildlight/Philip Quirk 42tl;
Woodfin Camp/Roger Werth 5cl, 8t.
Jacket credit: Corbis/Jim Sugar (photography)

Contents

DK ELT Graded Readers

INTERMEDIATE

VOLCANOES

Written by
Michael Potter

Series Editor Susan Holden

DK

London • New York • Delhi • Sydney

Floodwater
A period of heavy rain can cause rivers to flood unexpectedly.

Planet Power!

Volcanoes, earthquakes, tidal waves, hurricanes, flash floods, and forest fires – when nature decides to go wild, she can be spectacular, but it can also be a terrifying experience.

In spite of all the modern resources that exist today, disasters caused by nature still manage to ruin people's lives. Sometimes the victims will never recover from the effects of the disaster.

Long Island, USA
(Hurricane, 1938)
A fierce storm brought huge waves towards the eastern coast of the United States (see pages 32–37).

Lisbon, Portugal
(Earthquake, 1775)
Earth tremors and fires destroyed large areas of Portugal's capital city (see pages 14–17).

PACIFIC OCEAN

NORTH AMERICA

ATLANTIC OCEAN

EUROPE

AFRICA

SOUTH AMERICA

San Francisco, USA
(Earthquake, 1906)
Much of the city was destroyed when buildings collapsed and fire broke out everywhere (see pages 26–31).

Yungay, Peru
(Avalanche, 1970)
In the mountains of Peru, an avalanche of ice and rock buried the people of Yungay alive (see pages 38–41).

Martinique, Caribbean
(Volcano, 1902)
The terrible eruption of Mount Pelée destroyed the port of St. Pierre (see pages 22–25).

Every year, disasters that are caused by nature kill and injure millions of people. Many others lose their homes and have nowhere to live. Nature can cause great suffering and hardship.

Here are the stories of some of the worst natural disasters that have happened in the history of the world. The map below shows you where the disasters happened, what kind of disaster they were, and where you can find them in the book. These are natural horror stories!

Hurricane winds
These winds can pull trees out of the ground, throw cars in the air like toys, and tear roofs off buildings.

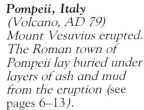

Pompeii, Italy
(Volcano, AD 79)
Mount Vesuvius erupted. The Roman town of Pompeii lay buried under layers of ash and mud from the eruption (see pages 6–13*).*

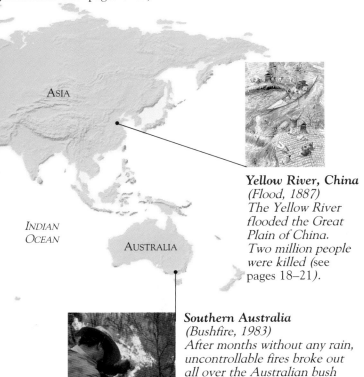

ASIA

INDIAN OCEAN

AUSTRALIA

Yellow River, China
(Flood, 1887)
The Yellow River flooded the Great Plain of China. Two million people were killed (see pages 18–21*).*

Southern Australia
(Bushfire, 1983)
After months without any rain, uncontrollable fires broke out all over the Australian bush (see pages 42–45*).*

Lava flow
Sometimes red-hot lava only flows gently from a volcano. But the lava can also be thrown high into the air when the volcano explodes.

Vesuvius
Farmers grew crops on the mountain. There was no reason to be afraid ... the volcano had been quiet for 800 years.

Take-away
At the outdoor cafes, there were big stone bowls in the counters. The food kept cool here.

Vesuvius Erupts!

ITALY, AD 79

It was an incredibly hot morning in August. The town of Pompeii, which lies at the foot of Mount Vesuvius in southern Italy, was full of people. They knew that Vesuvius was a volcano but it had not erupted for years. It was inactive ... perhaps even extinct.

In spite of the heat, the streets and markets were very busy. Farmers were bringing fresh fruit and vegetables from their fields on the slopes of the mountain in carts that were pulled by donkeys. There were grapes and figs in the markets, and people were choosing the best ones, and arguing about the prices. A group of travelling musicians was playing, and everyone felt happy and relaxed.

At a take-away restaurant, two women ordered snacks for their children. A man who had tied his dog to the counter was waiting to be served. They were all feeling hungry.

In the packed bars, the people were talking excitedly about the games they could watch in the amphitheatre that afternoon. This was a very large stadium where huge crowds could watch fierce sports. They could see gladiators fighting each other ... and often killing each other! The crowds loved blood and violence. They were always bloodthirsty, and the hot sun made them feel even more bloodthirsty! And, after all, most of the gladiators were criminals who were being punished for their crimes. Surely, they deserved to die!

Just then, the ground trembled. The women at the take-away counter looked at each other. They looked worried. Could it be an earthquake? Earthquakes were common in this area, but they were usually small, and did little damage. If this was an earthquake, it would be the same. The women smiled at each other.

Suddenly, there was a deafening bang ... and the top of Mount Vesuvius disappeared!

Gladiator helmet
Gladiators were criminals or slaves. The most successful fighters could win their freedom if they killed enough opponents.

Amphitheatre
Gladiator fights and chariot races took place in the amphitheatre in Pompeii.

Blast-off!
Hot, liquid rock moved up through the volcano. Then, the lava exploded through the top of the mountain.

Unlucky wind
The force of the eruption broke the hot rock into billions of pieces of ash. Wind blew the deadly cloud of ash towards Pompeii.

Mount Vesuvius, which had remained quiet for so many years, was erupting. A fountain of fire shot high into the air. Huge black clouds rose hundreds of metres up into the sky.

When they saw what was happening, the people were terrified. The force of the explosion threw them across the street. Some managed to cling tightly to a pillar or another person.

A volcanic eruption hurls huge clouds of ash into the sky.

The women at the take-away grabbed their children and held them tightly to their bodies. The dog that the man had tied to the counter, began to bark wildly. It pulled at its lead in a desperate attempt to get free and run away. The streets were full of people who were trying to find a safe place to hide. There was a lot of confusion and panic as people ran out of their houses and the shops and bars.

The great clouds of ash and smoke covered the sun and everything became dark in Pompeii. Flashes of lightning zigzagged through the cloud of ash that towered above Mount Vesuvius. There was a noise of strong wind, and people crying and shouting.

Hot, burning ash and rocks – some bigger than tennis balls – fell like heavy rain down from the sky. In the town, crowds of people ran shouting and screaming through the dark streets. They ran here, they ran there; they had no idea where they might be safe from the rocks and ash. They knocked over the stalls that people had set up in the market. Fruit and vegetables spilled all over the street. They were crushed as the terrified crowd ran and slipped over them. Even the gladiators who were training for their fights in the amphitheatre dropped their weapons and ran.

Some people rushed into their homes and grabbed jewels, money and other precious objects. Others tried to protect themselves from the hot ash and grabbed cushions or towels which they tied to their heads before they tried to escape from the town. No one really knew what to do.

Eyewitness
A man named Pliny watched the eruption from a distance. This description of the explosion comes from Pliny's account of the disaster.

Raging sea
The water in the nearby Bay of Naples began to boil when the hot rocks and ash fell into the sea.

9

The hot ash was falling everywhere. It stuck in people's throats and water began to fall from their eyes. They could only breathe with great difficulty and coughed and spat. But it was no use. People began to collapse in the street. Their clothes soon became covered with a thick layer of ash. When they tried to brush it off a new layer quickly formed! Their clothes became heavier and heavier. Their breathing became more and more difficult.

Everyone was terrified. One man shouted, "The gods are angry with us! This is the end of the world!"

Another man went down on to his knees and raised his arms in the air. He was praying to the gods to help him and to help Pompeii. "Have pity on us," he cried out.

The ash piled up deeper and deeper. Soon, many of the streets were blocked. Nobody could pass down them any more. The ash began to fill the rooms of the empty houses, and their roofs started to collapse because of the great weight of the ash and rock that had fallen on them.

The air was thick with ash and poisonous fumes; it was impossible to breathe properly any more. The town was quickly disappearing under what looked like a thick blanket of grey snow.

The streets that led out from Pompeii were full of people hurrying away from the city. Some were pushing carts with the things that they could rescue. Others were pulling terrified animals, or holding crying children. No one knew if the countryside would be safer, but they wanted to get away from the city and its falling buildings … and the terrible fumes and ash.

About 2,000 people remained in Pompeii or were unable to escape from the town. They all died. Most of them suffocated when they breathed in the deadly ash, or were crushed by falling buildings. But more than 20,000 people managed to escape to the countryside nearby.

In less than two days, the town was buried under 4.5–6 metres (15–20 feet) of ash and rocks. After the eruption, heavy rain began to fall on the ash which became hard like cement. The town of Pompeii remained under its rocky tomb for the next 1800 years.

Roman gods
The Romans worshipped many gods and goddesses. Venus (above) was Pompeii's most important goddess.

Volcanic ash
The eruption of Vesuvius threw ash very high into the air. Some of the ash landed in Africa and Syria!

Burned toast
Eighty-one loaves of bread, which were ready for people to eat on that day in AD 79, were found in a baker's oven.

In 1860, the king of Italy brought together a team of archaeologists and sent them to uncover Pompeii. When they began to remove the layers of rock, the archaeologists looked in amazement. The town did not look different from the day of the eruption. It was a town that was frozen in time. A pile of coins lay on the counter of a bar, pots and pans stood on a cooking stove. They even found a bowl of eggs that someone had placed on a table.

They also found that the bodies of the people of Pompeii, who had died in the disaster, had rotted away and disappeared. But their bodies had left behind an almost perfect hollow outline of their shape in the rock.

This dog lies curle up in great pain. He is still wearing his bronze collar and chain.

This cast shows a mother who is trying to protect her child from the ash.

The archaeologists poured wet plaster into the hollow shapes and made models of the bodies. These models were called casts. When the plaster had become hard, the archaeologists cut carefully around the surrounding rock and removed the casts. The

casts show the people at the very last moment of their lives. Many of them are covering their faces, trying to protect their children, gripping a bag of jewels, or covering another terrified person with their arms and body.

Pompeii today
Today, you can walk along the streets of ancient Pompeii.

The eruption of Vesuvius was a terrible event. But the remarkable way in which the town, and the people who remained there, were frozen at the moment of their destruction with everything that they owned or used, means that, today, we have a unique and exceptional record of how the Romans lived at that time.

Pompeii is a kind of museum, or a waxworks, with the people and their animals frozen in time. Or perhaps it is like some terrible fairy story, where everyone is sleeping, and waiting for some magic to wake them up again.

Frightening reminder
This picture of a skull is from a house in Pompeii. Skulls like this one reminded people that they should enjoy life while they could.

Mount Vesuvius is still an active volcano. It has erupted forty times since AD 79. And its history of death and destruction could still continue. In 1631, for example, there was another violent eruption and 18,000 people died. The most recent eruption was in 1944. Can we be sure that it will not decide to wake up again?

Lisbon
This is Lisbon today. In 1775, 275,000 people lived in the city. It was the centre of Portugal's empire which extended as far as South America and China.

Galleons
These huge ships brought precious cargoes of gold, silver, silk, and spices from all over the empire.

Lisbon's Great Quake

PORTUGAL, 1755

It was a quiet, peaceful day in Lisbon, the capital city of Portugal and the centre of Portugal's great empire. Down in the city's harbour, mighty merchant ships, called galleons, rose and fell gently on the waves. They had come with precious goods from all parts of the world. Their cargoes were already safely delivered to the merchants' warehouses near the harbour. But today nobody was working. It was a holiday and the streets were empty. People were celebrating the festival of All Saints Day. They were in church praying for friends and relatives who had died.

In the royal chapel, where King José and his family were praying, everything was still and quiet. Even the flames of the candles on the altar did not move. The smell of incense filled the air.

Suddenly, there was a frightening rumbling noise and the ground began to shake. The shaking soon stopped and everything became calm. Then there was another rumble and the earth trembled again. This time, the shaking lasted for two full minutes. It was the beginning of an earthquake. You couldn't mistake the noise or the shaking!

All over the city, church spires were swaying from one side to the other, just like corn swaying in the wind. Inside the churches, the bells clanged as they were thrown forwards and backwards, to the left and to the right. Like the bells, hanging lights full of burning candles also started to swing madly.

Large pieces of stone fell from buildings onto the ground below. Other buildings first began to sway and shake and then, suddenly crashed to the ground. Many people were crushed to death under the collapsed buildings.

A third tremor came. It threw clouds of dust into the air. It was like a fog. People couldn't see anything and were running and screaming in all directions. Inside the royal chapel, statues fell off the walls and altars crashed to the floor. The ceiling of the chapel began to collapse. But the King and his family managed to escape before the roof finally fell. Everybody was trying to get away from the centre of the city. They were all running towards the harbour where there were no buildings. But, even at the harbour, they were not going to be safe.

King José I
José I was King of Portugal from 1750 to 1777.

15

Giant waves
The giant waves that struck Lisbon's harbour were 15 metres (50 feet) high.

Destruction
Buildings that survived the quake were destroyed by raging fires.

When the crowds reached the harbour, they could not believe what they saw. The shock waves from the earthquake had pulled the sea back half a mile from the shore. Then the sea rose up to a great height and three giant waves crashed towards the shore. There was no way for people to escape. The waves caught the mighty galleons in the harbour and threw them like little pieces of wood against the shore. Then, they crashed over the harbour and against the collapsing buildings. They swept over the fleeing crowds and dragged them back into the sea.

Many buildings caught fire when candles, that had fallen over during the earthquake, set alight the wooden beams of buildings that had collapsed. The fire spread rapidly from building to building. Soon the whole city was on fire. Lisbon was almost destroyed.

King José and his family managed to escape safely. But 60,000 people died in the earthquake. Before the disaster there were more than 20,000 houses in the city. Now, only 3,000 houses remained.

Scientists became very interested in what had happened in Lisbon. At that time, many people believed that earthquakes were caused by God, when He wanted to punish the world. Now, for the first time, scientists were suggesting that earthquakes were natural events that happened because of movements inside the earth.

Poor peasants
Peasants own land but they are poor. They work on their land, grow crops, and look after their animals.

Yellow River
The river winds its way through northern China towards the Yellow Sea. It is called the Yellow River because of the colour of the clay that it carries.

River of Sorrow

NORTHERN CHINA, 1887

Life was very difficult for the Chinese peasant farmers who lived near the mighty Yellow River. They used to work in the fields below the river from early in the morning to late in the evening – all day, every day! But they still could not produce enough food to feed their families. The land was poor.

For hundreds of years, the Yellow River had flooded the flat lands of China's Great Plain. The plain had flooded more than 1,500 times. People used to call the river "China's Sorrow" because of the large number of deaths and terrible suffering that it had caused to those who lived near its banks during these floods.

The peasants knew that the river was dangerous, but they always hoped they would be lucky. Each year, they hoped that the floods would not come. They needed water for their crops, so some rain was good. Each year, they watched the level of the water in the river carefully.

In September 1887, the rain didn't stop. It poured and poured down all day and night. The river began to rise and people were afraid that it might cause another flood.

In spite of the fear of flooding, nobody wanted to leave. This was where they lived and where their families had lived for hundreds of years. Why should they leave? And it was harvest time - if they didn't bring in their crops soon, they would have no food for the winter. They and their families would starve.

The peasants had a terrible choice. Stay, and face the possibility of flooding. Or go, and face the prospect of starvation. And where could they go? Perhaps it was better to stay in your own village and bring in your crops. Perhaps the rain would stop. Perhaps the river would not continue to rise.

The rain continued to fall and the river rose higher and higher. In some places the river was already 5 metres (15 feet) higher than the flat lands that lay below its banks. But the peasants knew their river! Those who were not helping to gather the harvest began to build dykes near the river's banks. These dykes had to be strong and secure because they were the only defence against the flood waters.

But it was hopeless. At a sharp bend near the city of Zhengzhou, the fast river finally burst over its banks. It made a gap in the dykes that stretched for over half a mile. Nothing could stop the torrent of water that poured onto the Great Plain.

Harvest crops
The peasants grew wheat, corn, rice, sweet potatoes, and a type of grass called sorghum.

Flood defence
For 2,500 years, the Chinese have built dykes and dug channels that take away the floodwater.

Rafts
The peasants' rafts were made out of straw and thin strips of wood. You can still see rafts like these on the Yellow River today.

Disease
Drinking water that was polluted by the flood caused sickness and disease.

Constant threat
After 1887, the river flooded many times. In 1991, 1,270 people drowned and 2 million lost their homes.

The noise was deafening. Peasants working in the fields were swept away by the rushing water. They cried out for help but nobody could hear their cries. The torrent soon reached the villages beyond the river. The water rose swiftly, and people climbed onto the roofs of their fragile houses for safety. Some managed to get into their boats or rafts. It was difficult for them to stay afloat in the raging waters. They had to look out for the fallen trees and dead cattle that were carried by the swift current. But those who were braver, even managed to rescue some people from their rooftops or throw some food as they passed by.

The flood covered 11 cities and killed 900,000 people. Thousands more people died of disease or because they had no food. It took 18 months to repair the dykes and to control the flow of the river.

This was one of the worst floods in China's history. The effect on the country was enormous. It taught people that they needed more efficient defences against the floods. The scientists learned from this flood and decided what to do.

Today, the flood defences along the Yellow River are much better than they used to be. Dynamite explosives were used to change the river's direction, particularly where there are dangerous bends like the one where the dyke broke in the great flood of 1887. There are also plans to build a huge, powerful dam. But nobody believes that it will be possible to completely control the river. "China's Sorrow" will surely claim many more victims.

Pelée Awakes

Mount Pelée
This mountain was named after Pele, the Hawaiian goddess of volcanoes. In 1852, a small eruption covered the mountain with grey ash.

MARTINIQUE, CARIBBEAN, 1902

It was nearly eight o'clock in the morning and the port of St. Pierre on the Caribbean island of Martinique was already very busy. Merchants were checking the cargoes of sugar, rum, and bananas that were being loaded onto ships. In the town, the shops were already open, and rich French tourists were walking up and down the elegant streets and looking at the beautiful displays of goods in the shop windows. Out in the countryside, it was already a hot and steamy day, and the local people were working hard picking fruit in the orchards or cutting bunches of green bananas in the plantations.

But something else was happening too. Down at the port, a large crowd of people was waiting for boats to take them off the islands. People were leaving the town with furniture and other possessions. Others were travelling on foot and carrying a few belongings in baskets on their heads.

At night, red-hot ash and lava from Mount Pelée lit up the sky.

Governor Mouttet stayed in the town. He wanted to show the people of St. Pierre that there was no danger.

They were nervous because a cloud of smoke and ashes was pouring out of the volcano, Mount Pelée, which had not been active for many years. Government authorities had made tests. They had wanted to know if there was any danger that the volcano might erupt. They said that there was no danger and that St. Pierre was safe. But this did not stop the people who were today leaving the town in greater and greater numbers. Everyone was afraid that the volcano was going to erupt. Governor Mouttet, who was responsible for the administration of the island, sent guards down to the port and the roads that led out of

town. He did not want any more people to leave. It was not good for the town, and he knew that there was no danger.

Leon, the local shoemaker, saw all the people who were trying to leave the city. He was not worried. He had lived in St. Pierre all his life and knew nothing was going to happen.

Prisoner Ciparis was a murderer who was sentenced to death by the island's criminal court.

23

Stopped watch
This watch stopped when it melted. It was 8.15 in the morning.

Bloodthirsty
The harbour of St. Pierre filled with hungry sharks that were attracted by the dead bodies floating in the water.

Locked in his prison cell, Auguste Ciparis knew of no reason why he should worry. He was locked in a small room where there wasn't even a window to look out of! He knew nothing about what was happening in the town. Suddenly, there was an enormous explosion like the sound of a thousand guns that were being fired at the same time. Mount Pelée had erupted. A fiery cloud of white-hot steam, dust, and poisonous gas started to roll down the mountain. It was heading directly towards St. Pierre.

The cloud was moving very fast. There was no time for people to escape. They knew that they did not have a chance! Most of them were killed instantly by the incredible heat and the poisonous gases in the air. The cloud was like a furnace. People's skulls and stomachs burst open as it passed over them.

Leon managed to get inside his house. He was clutching his chest. He felt a terrible sharp pain in his lungs and his skin was burning. He pulled himself into his bedroom and threw himself on his bed. He was sure that he was going to die. The heat became fiercer and fiercer. Everywhere around him, things were beginning to melt or catch fire.

A river of burning rum, from warehouses that were now flat ruins, was flowing down the streets. The fiery blast swept over the harbour where it threw ships over onto their sides and sank them as it passed. In only a few seconds, St. Pierre had become a flaming ruin!

Glass wine bottle

Melting
Temperatures in the cloud rose to 1,000° C (1,800°F). The heat melted objects like the wine bottle above.

Amazingly, Leon survived. Rescuers searched the whole town, but they did not find any other survivors. Leon was the only survivor - or that was what everybody thought at the time! Four days later, the rescuers heard a faint cry. They pulled away all the fallen stones and managed to make a large hole in the wall of the building. Imagine their surprise when they found Ciparis alive and well inside! The thick walls had saved his life! Because of his remarkable escape from the eruption, Ciparis was later pardoned by the court and became a free man.

The eruption of Mount Pelée was the twentieth century's worst volcanic disaster. Only two people survived. The rest of St. Pierre's 30,000 citizens were killed in only a few minutes and never lived to tell the story.

Iron nails

Spoon and fork

San Francisco
Before 1850, San Francisco was just a collection of huts and small buildings. But the city became rich because of the American gold rush.

Chinatown
Many Chinese workers lived in Chinatown. They formed the largest Chinese community outside Asia.

Earthquake!

SAN FRANCISCO, USA, 1906

The Sun was beginning to rise over the city of San Francisco. Carl and Pedro were two tourists who were walking slowly back to their hotel. They had just spent an enjoyable night out in a district of the city called Chinatown. They had enjoyed the delicious Chinese food and had been to a show where they had seen jugglers and a Chinese lion-dance.

The two friends were laughing and joking about the fun that they had had that evening. "Wow! What a night we've had!" said Pedro, "I think I'm going to sleep all day!" Suddenly, Carl seemed to throw himself against a wall. "Hey! Stop fooling around!" shouted Pedro. Then, he, too, was thrown onto the ground. He could feel the earth shaking and heaving under him.

Bricks and pieces of broken glass fell into the street. The buildings around them started to lean over and sway dangerously.

A terrified man ran past them. "Run! Run!" he cried. "It's a quake, it's a quake."

Carl and Pedro looked at each other. Where could they go? They were tourists in a strange city.

The noise of the earthquake was strange and horrifying. The two young friends listened to the earth as it shook, groaned, and rumbled under them. They could also hear the screams of terrified people as they rushed out of their collapsing houses. Most of the people were still wearing their night clothes.

The tremors did not go on for a long time. After a few minutes they stopped. Carl and Pedro stood up and did not believe what they saw. The earthquake had flattened whole streets. Not a single building was still standing. Even City Hall, which everyone had said could survive any earthquake, was almost a complete ruin. The city looked completely different. Carl and Pedro could not recognize anything. It was like a bad dream.

City Hall
The dome of the hall still remained. Luckily, the steel girders that supported it did not collapse.

Ham and Eggs Fire
One of the worst fires was the "Ham and Eggs Fire". It began when a woman was cooking breakfast in her damaged home.

Fire engines
The city's 38 fire engines were pulled by horses. There were not enough fire engines to fight the 52 fires that broke out in San Francisco.

This was not the first time that the people of San Francisco had experienced an earthquake. Small tremors were always happening. The city sits on the San Andreas Fault, which is a great crack in the Earth's surface. Two layers of the Earth's skin meet at this fault. These layers are called plates and they slide against each other. Sometimes, when they touch each other more strongly, they cause earthquakes.

It was very difficult for Carl and Pedro to find the street where their hotel was. Finally, they found the street, but they didn't find the hotel! In its place was just a pile of stones and rubble. All the other people who were staying at the hotel were killed when the building collapsed. Carl and Pedro were the only survivors.

The tremors had stopped, but this was only the beginning. The earthquake had broken all the pipes that took gas to the city's houses and buildings. Gas was escaping from the broken pipes into the streets. Fires started when the flames from stoves and heaters, or sparks from electricity cables that had also broken during the earthquake, came into contact with the gas. Loud explosions could be heard as the gas caught fire. Soon, whole streets were in flames.

There weren't enough firefighters to put out the fires that were breaking out everywhere. The earthquake had destroyed the pipes that supplied water to the city. The firefighters had to go down into the tunnels that took away the city's sewage and use the sewage water to fight the flames. In some restaurants, the owners were desperately trying to put out the fires with their precious wine

Because they didn't have enough water, the firefighters had to think how they could control the fires. They decided to blow up entire streets with dynamite to create fire breaks – gaps between buildings that would keep the flames away from areas that were not burning. But in spite of their desperate efforts, the fires were still spreading.

Fire breaks
When the firefighters blew up buildings to stop the fires, the explosions started more fires.

The fires destroyed more buildings than the earthquake.

29

Looters
Thieves looked through the rubble for jewels and other valuable objects. Some thieves were shot by police when they caught them.

Finally, the fires burned out. Only 500 people had died, but 200,000 people had lost their homes. They slept in the streets or in the city's parks and built shelters from pieces of wood, metal, or cardboard – anything that they could find. Some people lived in these shelters or tents for nearly three years. Some women even gave birth to their babies on the grass in the parks. The earthquake changed everybody's lives. But people did not give up. They were determined to build their city again.

People searched the rubble for their belongings.

They began to rebuild the city immediately. After four years, it was difficult to find any sign of the destruction that the earthquake had caused.

San Francisco still suffers from earthquakes. In 1994, a quake killed 61 people. But, today, it is possible to construct buildings that can resist the tremors. Firefighting technology has also improved considerably since 1906. Nowadays, San Francisco doesn't have to be rebuilt after each earthquake.

Temporary stoves
While they waited for the electricity supply to be restored, people prepared their meals on temporary stoves.

Camps
Thousands of people lived in tents for nearly three years after the earthquake.

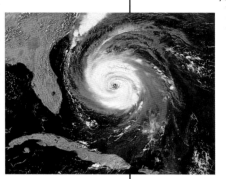

Wind speed
The hurricane travelled at 96 kilometres per hour (60 miles per hour), but wind speeds reached 290 kph (180 mph).

Storm-free
No hurricanes had struck Long Island for 100 years.

Long Island Express

NORTH-EASTERN USA, 1938

It was going to be a busy day for Janice Kelly. She was sitting at her home in Long Island on the north-eastern coast of the United States and was planning all the things that she had to do that day. She liked listening to the radio, which she always switched on early in the morning. She didn't listen carefully to everything that she heard.

Today, there was a weather report about a hurricane that was heading towards Florida. She was happy that she didn't live there; there were always hurricanes in Florida. Janice was more worried about rats than hurricanes far, far away! She hated rats; they made her nervous and there were lots of them running around down in the basement. She was going to tell her husband that he must buy some poison to kill them.

Down in Florida, people had heard the hurricane warning. It was the season for hurricanes, and they knew what they had to do. They started to cover the windows and doors of their houses to protect them against the powerful wind and rain. Then they made sure that they could find a safe place to stay during the storm.

But, suddenly, the hurricane changed direction. At first, it seemed that it was heading away from the coast and out to sea where it could cause no damage. Then it turned towards the north.

The hurricane was moving faster on its way to the north, and the winds were getting stronger. It raced towards Long Island and the north-eastern states of the United States like an express train. People were not expecting a hurricane and had not prepared themselves for what was going to happen. Homes were flattened, and even tall skyscrapers began to collapse under the force of the wind and driving rain. Many people were killed or injured by falling rubble.

Flying houses
In Madison, Connecticut, one house was lifted up and blown half a mile. Not a single window was broken!

Terrified people ran away from the falling buildings.

Windy city
The force of the hurricane winds in New York was very strong. Even the mighty Empire State Building began to sway.

The first place that the hurricane hit was Long Island. Lots of families had gone to the beach to relax and enjoy a day out at the seaside with their children. They sat on the beach eating their picnics and watching the children building sand castles. Nobody was swimming in the sea because the waves were quite large. But this did not worry the people on the beach. They did not know what was happening far out at sea. The strong wind was whipping up huge waves, which were moving towards the shore. The sky was becoming dark. A storm was on its way. People started to pack up their picnics and leave the beach or stopped to look at the big waves.

Suddenly a gigantic wave appeared. It was already very close to the shore. A huge wall of water 12 metres (40 feet) high crashed down on to the beach. Nobody had time to escape and everyone was swept away.

The sea poured over the beaches and into the countryside. No town or village along the coast escaped the force of the water and the storm. People were thrown into the floodwaters and desperately tried to save themselves. Some were rescued by people living in higher buildings who let down ropes made from bedsheets and pulled their neighbours safely out of the flood.

Hurricane winds blasted across seven states. Trains were thrown off the railway tracks. The floodwaters tore up roads and set off car horns. The sharp wails of the horns joined the screams of the raging winds. The noise was terrible.

Off the rails
This train was surrounded by seawater and began to sink. Luckily, all the passengers escaped.

Flood damage
This road was torn up when floodwater washed away the soil beneath it.

Wave power
In some places, the force of the waves changed the shape of the coastline forever.

Destruction
The winds and the tidal wave that they caused destroyed more than 57,000 houses. About 275 million trees were also destroyed.

Janice Kelly was nearly one of the victims of the hurricane that no one expected. Luckily, she heard the crash of the floodwaters that were rushing towards her house. She ran up the stairs with her husband and escaped on to the roof. But they were not the only ones to seek safety there. Three rats and a snake had got there before them! Janice trembled. She hated rats! But the raging storm terrified her even more.

The water was rising quickly and the roof was shaking violently in the wind. Janice threw one arm around her husband and the other around a roof beam. They were nearly blown off the fragile, rattling roof. Then with a loud ripping sound, the wind tore the roof off the house! Somehow Janice and her husband managed to cling on to the roof. They did not think that they were going to survive.

Suddenly, they were not in the air any more. The roof had fallen onto a golf course. The Kellys picked themselves off the ground. Surprisingly, they were not injured. They looked across the bay towards the house where they once used to live. What they saw was unbelievable! Houses were flattened; cars were lying on their sides or on their roofs in pools of mud; and nearly all the trees had been torn up from the ground. The Kellys had had an amazing escape on their unexpected life raft. Even their uninvited passengers, the rats and the snake, had managed to survive this terrifying experience!

The hurricane ruined the lives of thousands of people. 60,000 people were left homeless. More than 600 people were dead. The "Long Island Express", which was the name that they gave to the hurricane, travelled for 523 km (325 miles) before it finally lost its strength and became calm. It was a terrifying experience.

Paint stripper
The force of the wind ripped the paint off cars and tore off the paint from the outside of houses. Only bare wood remained.

Sea-salt
Wind carried sea-salt 193 km(120 miles) inland, where the salt made the windows white.

Andes
This huge wall of mountains stretches along the entire South American coast of the Pacific Ocean.

Peru's people
Peruvians are descendants of the ancient Inca people.

Rising higher
The Andes range of mountains is getting higher. This is because of movements inside the earth. One day, the Andes may be the highest mountain range in the world.

Avalanche

PERU, SOUTH AMERICA, 1970

It was the end of May and a group of Japanese friends were on a climbing holiday in Yungay. Yungay was a small but busy tourist resort that sat at the foot of Mount Huascarán in the Andes mountains of Peru. The people of Yungay, like most Peruvians, and most people who live in South America, love watching and playing football. And the World Cup football championship had just begun. Like people in other countries in South America, they were sure that their country was going to win the championship!

The Japanese friends liked climbing up the mountains to watch the sun rise over the Andes. Every day, they used to get up early and climb a different mountain to get a new view of the sunrise. At night, they enjoyed sitting under the giant palm trees in the town square and listening to the excited talk of the townspeople. Most of the conversations that they heard were probably about the Peruvian World Cup football team!

One afternoon, when the friends were climbing in the mountains near the city, a tremendous earthquake ripped open the ocean bed near the Peruvian coast. There were terrific waves in the sea. Earth tremors rippled across the country and towards the Andes mountains.

The tremors reached Yungay 23 minutes after the beginning of the first World Cup game. Most people were watching the match on television at home or in the town's bars and cafes.

The Japanese friends didn't really understand football, and they had decided to climb up Mount Huascarán to enjoy the beautiful mountain scenery. They sat down and looked down at the quiet town. It seemed peaceful, but, at that time everyone was shouting and screaming wildly as they watched the football game in the bars and cafes! The climbers heard a low rumbling sound. They were not worried. Perhaps a few rocks were falling down the mountain. But the noise seemed to become louder and louder.

Then, far below them, the mountainside started to move. They looked down. What they saw was terrifying! A huge avalanche of ice and rock was rolling down the mountain. It was heading directly towards the town.

39

The climbers saw giant rocks larger than houses bouncing down the mountain slope. They were part of a great wall of ice, mud, and stone that hit the town and buried it.

They hurried down the mountainside to look for survivors. But, when they reached the town, they realized that there was nothing that they could do. Yungay did not exist any more. All that they could see were the tops of the giant palm trees in the town square. The only survivors were a few people who were visiting a cemetery on the top of a nearby hill when the avalanche hit the town.

Yungay was not the only town that the earthquake destroyed. Other towns and villages also suffered. Many of the smaller villages were, now, only a pile of stones and rubble. The whole world was horrified by the size of this terrible disaster.

In South America, football is so important that it can help people to forget some of the disasters of their everyday lives.

A short time later, Peru won its World Cup match against Bulgaria. Winning the match helped to give the people the courage that they needed to rebuild their shattered lives.

Rescue
Three days after the avalanche, the mud was hard enough for help to get to Yungay.

The statue of Jesus in the cemetery was the only thing not destroyed by the avalanche. 41

Bush
The bush is uncultivated land that is covered with low bushes and trees.

Eucalyptus
These trees burn quickly because their leaves are full of oil.

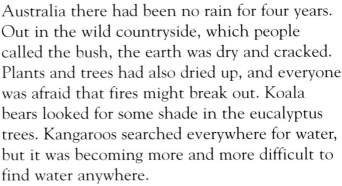

Bushfire

AUSTRALIA, 1983
It was the hottest February that people could remember. In some parts of southern Australia there had been no rain for four years. Out in the wild countryside, which people called the bush, the earth was dry and cracked. Plants and trees had also dried up, and everyone was afraid that fires might break out. Koala bears looked for some shade in the eucalyptus trees. Kangaroos searched everywhere for water, but it was becoming more and more difficult to find water anywhere.

Alan and Judy Watts lived on a farm near to the city of Melbourne. They looked out at their dry fields. "I'm worried," said Judy. "There have been fire warnings on the radio all day." The radio is very important in Australia, where the distances between towns are often enormous. It helps people to communicate.

Out in the bush, the sun was very hot indeed. The grass and trees could not tolerate the heat any more. There was no more moisture in the ground to protect them. Little by little, smoke began to appear, and soon the bush was in flames. The hot wind helped to spread the fires. Small fires soon became large ones, and even the trees began to burst into flames.

Firefighters and groups of local people who were called "bush brigades" fought to control the raging fires.

Soon, despite the firefighters' efforts, a wall of fire that was more than 15 metres high was rolling over the land. It was travelling at speeds of more than 113 kilometres per hour!

The Watts family saw the dark, dusty smoke that was heading towards them. What could they do to protect themselves? In only a few minutes, their home was surrounded by a gigantic wall of flames. Huge balls of fire and flame jumped across the road that led to the farmhouse. Alan and Judy had to think fast. They knew that they couldn't escape. Buy they had to do something. If they didn't, they would be killed.

Bush brigades
These firefighters carry water packs and beaters, which look like spades, to put out the flames.

Ash clouds
In Melbourne, ash from the fire formed a thick crust on the surface of swimming pools.

A safe place
The metal sides of the water tank protected the family from the flames.

"We've got only one chance - get in the water tank now!" shouted Judy. The flames were now very close. She rushed into the house and grabbed her baby and three older children. The children had poured water on some sheets and had covered their heads with the sheets. They ran to the huge water storage tank near the house, where Alan was waiting for them. He helped Judy and the children to scramble up the ladder and climb into the tank. The wall of the tank was very high. They couldn't see the fire, but they could hear it. They listened to the terrifying crackle of the fire as it burnt up all the trees in the forest.

The fire swirled around the water tank. Inside the tank, the water was getting hotter and the Watts family was feeling more and more uncomfortable. "We're going to be boiled alive!" thought Alan.

Finally, the fire passed by and the water began to get cooler. But the Watts family waited for ten hours before they pulled themselves out of the tank. They were weak and completely exhausted. The air was still full of smoke, but they could see that their house was destroyed. Hundreds of dead farm animals lay on the black burnt-out land. The Watts family couldn't believe that they had survived. They were just grateful that they were still alive.

About 70 people did not have the same luck. A man, his wife, and three children died in a car when they tried to race away from the flames. Twelve firefighters were surrounded by flames and could not escape. The fire caused great damage wherever it passed. It destroyed seven towns and left 8,500 people homeless. More than 200,000 sheep and cattle were killed by the flames. Thousands of kangaroos and koala bears must have died in the fire, too. The animals were trapped and helpless.

Many Australians are farmers, who depend on their sheep and cattle to earn their living. So, many families were ruined economically, even if they were not killed by the fire.

The bushfire of 1983 was the worst fire in Australia's history.

Burned earth
60,702 hectares (150,000 acres) of land were burned black by the fires.

Refugees
Temporary camps were built for people who were left homeless by the fire.

Dealing with Disasters

RESCUE OPERATIONS – A RACE AGAINST TIME
After a big disaster, rescue operations are often difficult and dangerous. Collapsed buildings crush many people to death, but a lot of people survive and are buried alive beneath the rubble. Flooded homes also separate a lot of people from the world around them. For rescuers, finding these survivors is a race against time.

Rescue Equipment

Trapped-person detector
When thousands of people are buried alive, this machine, which detects movement, can help to find survivors. This equipment helped to save hundreds of lives after the earthquake in Armenia in 1988.

Thermal image camera
This camera is used after all kinds of disasters. It can detect the heat of a living person.

Sniffer dogs
These dogs receive special training. They can find survivors who are buried by mud or rubble.

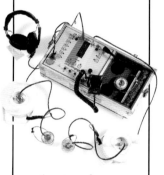

This survivor was rescued after a volcano erupted in Colombia in 1985.

A microphone helps rescuers to talk to a person who is trapped.

The controls show if heat is present.

46

Preparing for Disasters

In parts of the world where disasters frequently happen, it is important to check the movement of volcanoes, fault lines, and the weather. People need time to prepare for what might happen. It is not possible to prevent natural disasters, but good planning and preparation can reduce some of their worst effects.

Shake it up
Buildings in parts of the world where earthquakes occur are designed to tolerate the deadly shaking. The Transamerica Pyramid in San Francisco looks fragile but its narrow-cone shape makes it stronger than a square-sided building.

Earthquake exercises
In Japan and California, earthquake exercises are part of daily life. Children learn to keep a torch and strong shoes at the side of their bed in case an earthquake strikes at night.

Transamerica Pyramid

Snow stoppers
Trees that are planted above a village are the oldest and best way to slow down an avalanche. Another way is to build a solid V-shaped stone wall, which can divide up an avalanche so that it avoids a village or building.

Glossary

amphitheatre
An open-air stadium. The ancient Romans watched gladiators fight in the amphitheatre.

archaeologist
A scientist who digs up ancient remains and tries to find out what happened in the past.

avalanche
A huge fall of rock, ice, and snow from the side of a mountain.

bush
An open, uncultivated area of grass, shrubs, and trees.

cast
A model that is made when plaster or liquid metal is poured into a hollow mould.

crust
The Earth's outer layer, made up of huge slabs of rock that lie on a bed of liquid rock.

drought
A long period with very little rain or no rain at all.

dyke
A wall that is built at the side of a river or canal to hold back floodwater.

earthquake
A shaking of the ground that happens when the plates that are part of the Earth's crust come into contact violently with each other.

eruption
The explosion of a volcano, which may throw out lava, steam, ash, dust, poisonous fumes, and hot gas.

fire break
A gap that is made by firefighters in a forest or between buildings to stop a fire when it begins to spread.

weather forecaster
A scientist who studies the weather and predicts how it will change.

galleon
A large sailing ship with three or four masts. Between the 15th and 18th centuries, galleons were used as warships and trading ships.

gladiator
A trained fighter in the ancient Roman empire, who fought against other gladiators or wild animals. The ancient Romans used to go to watch gladiators at the amphitheatre.

governor
A person who administers a place for another country.

hurricane
A terrible storm with a swirling mass of powerful winds at its centre.

incense
Special sticks that give off fragrant fumes when they are burned.

lava
Red-hot liquid rock that bursts from inside the Earth onto the surface.

looters
People who steal things from the scene of a disaster.

natural disaster
A destructive event that is caused by the forces of nature.

plain
A large expanse of level land in the open country.

plates
Segments of the Earth's crust. These large pieces of rock cover the Earth's surface like a giant jigsaw puzzle.

skyscraper
A very tall building, usually made of concrete and steel.

tremor
A trembling of the ground. Earthquakes occur when a number of powerful tremors happen one after the other.

volcano
A mountain where hot gases, ash, and liquid rock sometimes burst out from its top.